GOD
AND
RECOVERY

VOLUME 3

DEVELOPMENT

A 90-DAY DEVOTIONAL TOWARDS A JOURNEY OF HEALING, RECOVERY AND RESTORATION WITH GOD

JOSIANE SOMO

Paperback edition
ISBN: 979-8-9990706-2-3

Published by Ingram Sparks Publishing, Austin TX, USA

TIMOTHY MARTIN
1960-2025

A Mentor, A Friend
A Man Of Integrity
Tough But Also Tenderhearted
Loving, Caring, Affectionate To All.

He Gave The World a Tremendous Gift:
His Legacy – A Life Of Service.

His Life Embodied The Core Message In This Devotional:
Total Surrender And Reliance On God For Every Aspect Of Life.
May We All Follow Suit.

Your Love And Kindness Will Never Be Forgotten Sir.

SCRIPTURE PERMISSIONS

Contents

INTRODUCTION

Matthew 9:17 (NLT) states, "And no one puts new wine into old wine skins. For the old skins would burst from the pressure, spilling the wine and ruining the skins. New wine is stored in new wine skins so that both are preserved."

This devotional book, inspired by the Holy Spirit, began based on my experience as a mental health professional in the addiction field. Thus, it started as the journey of many men and women towards recovery from addiction to substances but, sadly, addiction is not limited to substances. Along the journey, it expanded with the ultimate goal: healing and restoration with our Lord.

In the book *Addiction and Grace*, Gerald May describes "addiction as a self-defeating force that abuses our freedom and makes us do things we really do not want to do". It is a state of compulsion, obsession, or preoccupation that enslaves a person's will and desire. As a result, displacing God's love as the source and object of our deepest true desire (May 1988).

Hence, this journey to healing, recovery, and restoration with God is a fight for our freedom from the hold these addictions have had. It is a journey we each must undertake, one on which each of us will be as we are perfected in Christ. It is a journey of death to self: meaning unless you can rid yourself of things holding you back, you may never reach your destination. You need new wine skins (a changed person and way of thinking) for you to be able to hold in the new wine: information, change, ideas and precepts.

This journey has been difficult and long for many due to the need to surrender, let go, be pruned, grow, forgive, and more. It also could have been difficult and long for many due to self-reliance, fear of the unknown, and impossibility mindset.

This devotional, inspired by the Holy Spirit, was written to show us how the Word of God can direct our path along this process. Note that the result is not as important as the person you must become during the process.

Are you ready to become who God created you to be so you could experience a better life, the one intended by God?

If yes, these ninety devotions will help you on this journey and give you tools that will strengthen you for the days ahead.

RUNNING YOUR RACE

1 CORINTHIANS 9:24–26 *(NLT)*

"Don't you realize that in a race everyone runs, but only one person gets the prize? So run to win! All athletes are disciplined in their training. They do it to win a prize that will fade away, but we do it for an eternal prize. So I run with purpose in every step. I am not just shadow boxing."

Society and human ambition have turned life into a competition, where people compare themselves and measure their progress against others. However, life is more like an Olympic race; success comes from focusing on your own lane and overcoming the hurdles in front of you, rather than being distracted by others.

Perhaps this is why the Apostle Paul, in Acts 20:24, emphasized the importance of fulfilling the unique work assigned to each of us by the Lord. We cannot measure our progress, or lack thereof, by comparing ourselves to others. When life feels chaotic, the first thing to evaluate is: Who set the course I'm running? Am I still in my lane?

A strong sense of identity makes it easier to recognize and stay in your own lane. Likewise, having a clear sense of purpose and vision helps you stay focused on your personal race. If life feels confusing or meaningless, could it be that you are not fully running the race set for you? Are you moving forward with clear intent?

The Apostle Paul urges us to "run with purpose in every step" (1 Cor. 9:26). Are you merely following the crowd, doing what everyone else is doing?

Remember, it is possible to finish a race yet miss the prize; simply because you were running the wrong one. This often looks like constantly hustling in different areas of life, yet never finding fulfillment because the effort never truly leads to completion.

What You Can Do:
- Discipline yourself: bring your body, mind, and emotions under control so that you do not fall short in the end.
- Reflect on why you are pursuing your current goals, whether it is a degree, a recovery journey, or a personal sacrifice.
- Set a goal that extends beyond personal gain, one that serves a greater purpose then run toward it with unwavering focus on Christ.

ASK YOURSELF

* Am I staying in my lane?

* Am I fulfilling what I am meant to do at this moment?

* Have I felt overwhelmed, out of balance, or as if everything is working against me?

DO NOT RUN ALONE

ECCLESIASTES 4: 9–10 *(ERV)*
*"Two people are better than one. When two people work
together, they get more work done. If one person falls, the
other person can reach out to help. But those who are alone
when they fall have no one to help them."*

Have you ever heard yourself or others say, "I do not trust people,
I would rather be alone; no one is there when I need them?" The
truth is, many people have experienced hardships that have left them
with a bitter taste when it comes to relationships. While this feeling is
understandable, it contradicts two fundamental truths: first, humans
are naturally social beings; second, it is much easier to rise after a fall
when you have support. Even the strongest among us: the spiritual, the
prophetic, those who always uplift others, still need encouragement,
guidance, and a listening ear.

Through life's experiences, it is evident that the enemy has successfully
planted a belief system that isolates us from the support we need.

Just as a predator easily targets an isolated animal, we become more vulnerable when we separate ourselves from our community.

This is why King Solomon, in his wisdom, wrote: "Two are better than one; when they work together, they achieve more. If one falls, the other lifts them up. But woe to the one who falls alone with no one to help". We are all working on something; whether it is recovery, emotional healing, marriage, or a personal project.

This verse reminds us that while we may accomplish things alone, having someone by our side makes the journey easier and more fulfilling. Having the right people in your life means having support, encouragement, and a voice that speaks life into you when you need it most.

ASK YOURSELF

* Who are my true friends?

* Who makes my journey smoother and encourages me along the way?

* Who offers me wisdom, holds me accountable, and helps me avoid costly mistakes?

* Who in my life has truly stood by me as a loyal friend?

* More importantly, have I been that kind of friend to someone else?

* What toxic habits or limiting beliefs have kept me from forming meaningful, destiny-shaping connections with the right people?

No matter what phase of life you are in, stop trying to do it all alone; we all need a strong, supportive community.

YOU WERE FORMED

PSALM 139:13 *(ERV)*
*"You formed the way I think and feel. You put me together in
my mother's womb."*

It is truly astonishing to consider how we were intricately crafted, like a masterpiece, and placed in our mothers' wombs. This thought never ceases to amaze me; it serves as a reminder of God's deep mindfulness toward each of us. The question is: How aware are you of this profound truth? What does it truly mean to be formed and intricately woven together?

Psalm 139:13 (ERV) highlights that God knows our thoughts and emotions intimately. Jeremiah 1:5 (TPT) further emphasizes that He knew us before we were formed and approved us as instruments in His hands. It is comforting to realize that nothing about us ever surprises the Lord. The disconnect often stems from our own lack of self-awareness.

We mistakenly believe we must navigate life alone, yet Jeremiah 33:3 assures us that if we call on Him, He will reveal the hidden things we do not recognize, understand, or know. Turning to the Lord for guidance illuminates the confusion in our lives and provides clarity. When you call on God, He will undoubtedly lead you; whether through a person with the answer you need, wise counsel for your next step, or another divine means.

Reflecting on our theme scripture, it is essential to remember that our formation in the womb was purposeful; we were created to be sent out by God and used for His glory. Have you discovered why you were uniquely formed? What recurring themes in your life reveal your purpose?

Keep in mind that this is the foundation upon which God evaluates your life. If you are uncertain about your purpose, Jeremiah 33:3 offers one way to discover it.

Another method is to identify recurring patterns and themes in your life over the years. Everything about us serves a purpose; whether it be marriage, recovery, business, writing, or life itself. Without a clear sense of purpose, it can be challenging to maintain stability in your identity and develop a focused vision for your life.

Another way to uncover your purpose is by being firmly anchored in your identity in Christ.

ASK YOURSELF

* Who am I at my core?

* What anchors my identity?

* How do I perceive God?

Your understanding of God profoundly influences your self-perception.

THE CALLED ARE EQUIPPED

HEBREWS 13:21 *(AMPC)*

"Strengthen (complete, perfect) and make you what you
ought to be and equip you with everything good that you
may carry out His will; [while He Himself] works in you and
accomplishes that which is pleasing in His sight, through Jesus
Christ (the Messiah); to Whom be the glory forever and ever
(to the ages of the ages). Amen (so be it)."

The phrase "God equips the called" is familiar to many of us, often heard in sermons and teachings. However, it is more than just a saying; it is a profound truth reinforced by scripture. Apostle Paul's prayer emphasizes that we may be strengthened, made complete, and fully equipped with everything good to fulfill God's will. As He works within us, He accomplishes what is pleasing in His sight through Jesus Christ. This is a powerful prayer with multiple layers, the most crucial being our willingness to allow God's equipping to take place.

Other important questions arise:
- Who are you meant to be in this season?
- What is God's will for your recovery, healing, marriage, career, family, or any other area of your life?

God's equipping aligns perfectly with His divine plan for you. Struggles often arise when we strive to fulfill our own desires rather than aligning with God's purpose. Feelings of inadequacy may surface, but take heart; God does not lie.

If He has declared you equipped, then you can trust that you are. God has already provided for you in every situation. However, recognizing and utilizing the right strategies or tools for effective results is a separate challenge. Your primary sources of guidance are the Holy Spirit and the Word of God. From there, God may lead you to additional tools that awaken the gifts within you. These tools may include books, conferences, training sessions, mentorship, therapy, and other valuable resources. Are you willing to set aside personal emotions, thoughts, and desires in order to align with the tools God has provided for your journey?

Until you fully submit and devote yourself to His will, life may continue to feel unsettled. Surrender and align with His plan; He will guide you to become all that you are meant to be. For clarity, God will not descend from heaven to guide you directly; instead, He will place the right teachers and mentors along your path (Jer. 3:15).

ASK YOURSELF

* Will I be able to recognize them?

* Will I align with God's will?

* Will I allow Him to work in and through me?

DEPRESSION

1 KINGS 19: 3–4 *(NLT)*

"Elijah was afraid and fled for his life. He went to Beersheba, a town in Judah, and he left his servant there. Then he went on alone into the wilderness, traveling all day. He sat down under a solitary broom tree and prayed that he might die. 'I have had enough, Lord,' he said. 'Take my life, for I am no better than my ancestors who have already died.'"

The term "depression" has become increasingly common in recent conversations. While some use it to describe feelings of sadness or being down, true depression runs much deeper, affecting a person's thoughts, emotions, behaviors, and overall well-being. Depression can be a lifelong struggle, a temporary phase, or a response to specific life events.

Common symptoms of depression include persistent sadness, irritability, emotional emptiness, loss of interest in previously enjoyed activities, difficulty concentrating, feelings of hopelessness or guilt, sudden drops in self-esteem, fatigue, and disruptions in eating or sleeping patterns (American Psychiatric Association, 2013).

Many individuals, particularly those regarded as the "strong friends," have mastered the art of masking their struggles. They show up, support others, share laughter, and even achieve great things, all while silently battling deep internal pain. They may be just one triggering event away from unraveling; much like Prophet Elijah in our theme scripture.

In the preceding chapter, Elijah had accomplished extraordinary feats: calling down fire from heaven, ending Israel's drought, and defeating the prophets of Baal.

However, in our theme scripture, a single event, the threat from Jezebel, sent Elijah spiraling into fear, self-doubt, loneliness, and even suicidal thoughts.

Elijah, despite his strength, faced depression and questioned his self-worth after not receiving the response he expected. This shows that life's challenges can affect anyone. The key to healing lies in what we turn to during these moments. Elijah poured out his heart to God, expressing his distress, and this openness can be a crucial step towards healing.

God's response was profoundly compassionate, rather than rebuking Elijah, He sent an angel to provide food and rest, preparing him for the journey ahead. God attended to his physical needs first. Contrary to common assumptions, sometimes the most spiritual act is simply to eat and rest. It is essential to nurture both your physical body and your spirit. It was not until he was nurtured that God inquired about his concerns; this provided comfort and safety.

This should pose as a template on how to help each other: be present, provide comfort and safety, then inquire. This sense of safety allowed Elijah to provide the reasons behind his current emotional state. God validated him; however provided him with what he needed; a personal encounter with him (1 Kgs. 19:11–12). That encounter was a reminder of the character of God; he felt seen and heard which is what we all long for in such circumstances. We need an outlet: a place of physical, soul, and spiritual replenishment but more importantly, we need to experience God's love, peace, and presence.

Are you experiencing a season like Elijah's; feeling alone, like a failure, and weighed down by negativity? Run to God, sit in His presence, unburden your heart to Him, and allow Him to restore you.

The beauty of God's response is that He doesn't just provide spiritual reassurance; He also acts practically. Just as He gave Elijah a new mission and a companion, Elisha, to walk alongside him, God provides support for our journeys as well.

ASK YOURSELF

(If you feel alone)

* Am I seeking God?

* Has He guided me to my tribe - a support support meant for me?

* Can I recognize this tribe?

Avoid chasing people based solely on emotions, as it may lead to disappointment.

WHAT ARE YOU REALLY ACCOMPLISHING HERE?

EXODUS 18:14 *(NLT)*

When Moses' father-in-law saw all that Moses was doing for the people, he asked, "What are you really accomplishing here? Why are you trying to do all this alone while everyone stands around you from morning till evening?

Have you ever felt overwhelmed by a project, task, or life role? Most of us take on leadership in some form, whether as a parent, boss, employee, older sibling, spouse, or even in managing our own lives. Have you ever paused to consider the ultimate goal of your efforts? What outcome do you hope to achieve? Is there a more efficient approach? Are you satisfied with your current results, or do the pressures and demands leave you feeling overwhelmed?

Many of us, like Moses, instinctively respond, "I have to do it, who else will?" Often, it takes an outside perspective to reveal our blind spots and inefficiencies. The responsibilities are undeniable, the recovery must continue, the children must be raised, the family must be supported, and the project must be completed. However, must you shoulder it all alone? And if so, how sustainable has that been? While Moses understood the people's need for divine guidance, he failed to see that carrying this burden alone was unsustainable, a truth Jethro pointed out. Recognizing this could be a turning point for many of us.

We must embrace guidance, help, and support. While certain responsibilities cannot be delegated, we should recognize the areas where we can lean on others. Delegation offers significant benefits: it allows you to concentrate on the most crucial matters and reveals the talents of those around you. Wisdom bridges the gap between recognizing what must be done and achieving the desired outcome.

ASK YOURSELF

* What is the most effective way to approach this?

* How can I lead my family with wisdom?

* How can I manage my leadership role at work?

* What is the best way to parent my children?

* How can I navigate recovery without feeling overwhelmed?

* What is my ultimate goal?

* If I was absent, could this process continue smoothly, or would confusion arise?

* Who can assist me?

* What is their capacity to help?

* What specific support do I need from them?

* Who is in my support system?

* How can I effectively utilize their help when I struggle?

* Who can offer counsel, guidance, or even a ride to a meeting?

* What can I delegate?

When people are involved in the process, they are less likely to criticize and more likely to contribute meaningfully. Consider recovery as an example; you cannot achieve sobriety alone. Regardless of your responsibilities, remember that you do not have to handle everything alone.

ANXIETY

PSALM 77:1–2 *(NIV)*
"I cried out to God for help; I cried out to God to hear me.
When I was in distress, I sought the Lord; at night I stretched
out untiring hands, and I would not be comforted."

Anxiety is commonly defined as a feeling of worry or nervousness, typically concerning an imminent event or an uncertain outcome (American Psychiatric Association, 2013). It manifests differently for everyone, making it crucial to recognize how it presents itself in your own life so you can address it effectively.

There are countless concerns that can fuel anxiety: our loved ones, life circumstances, financial burdens, upcoming events, and even past experiences. Fortunately, the Bible provides a powerful example of someone who struggled with anxiety. Throughout the book of Psalms, King David candidly expresses a range of emotions, including anxiety, uncertainty, fear, overwhelm, guilt, and shame.

For this discussion, we will focus specifically on anxiety. It has the ability to consume your entire being: your thoughts, emotions, body, and heart, leaving you feeling trapped and overwhelmed. The book of Psalms serves as an intimate glimpse into King David's personal reflections, much like a diary where he processed his emotions through writing. This highlights that journaling is not a new practice but rather an ancient and powerful tool.

David documented his experiences, emotions, and desires while intentionally inviting God into his struggles. He also reminded himself of past victories in moments of distress (Psa. 77). Remembering past triumphs can provide the strength needed to persevere.

Anxiety can feel even more overwhelming when it seems like no one understands or is there to support you. Many of us have experienced this isolation. Thankfully, God is always present, offering us comfort if we lean on Him (Psa. 94:19 NIV).

We can seek this peace by reflecting on scripture, practicing deep breathing, and embracing stillness. Psalm 55:22 (NIV) encourages us to cast our cares; whether they involve hurtful words, deadlines, relapse struggles, legal issues, relationships, or family concerns upon God, trusting that He will sustain us. While this may not always bring an immediate solution, it often provides a deep sense of relief.

Whether through journaling (writing or voice recording), speaking with a counselor or trusted friend, engaging in prayer and worship, or reading the Bible, you may experience the weight of anxiety begin to lift.

This practice fosters enough tranquility to help you process situations more clearly, seek solutions, and recognize when to ask for help.

ASK YOURSELF

* What has been weighing on my mind, causing unrest in my soul (thoughts, emotions, imagination), body, or life?

When you feel overwhelmed, I encourage you to lay your burdens before God; whether through writing, speaking, or another means that resonates with you. God may not physically descend to fix your situation, but He sustains us in countless ways: through people, through an inexplicable inner peace, or through the gentle whisper of wisdom when we quiet ourselves. Will you trust Him today?

WHERE ARE YOU?

GENESIS 3:9–10 *(NLT)*

"Then the Lord God called to the man, 'Where are you?' He replied, 'I heard you walking in the garden, so I hid. I was afraid because I was naked.'"

The question "Where are you?" is often used to determine a person's physical location, but it carries a much deeper meaning when used for self-reflection.

As you reflect, ponder on these:
- Where am I emotionally, mentally, physically, spiritually, and behaviorally?
- In other words, what events have shaped you, and where have they led you?

This passage recounts the well-known moment when Adam and Eve disobeyed God by eating from the forbidden tree. Sin is the act of disregarding God's instructions, whether revealed through prayer, Scripture, or wise counsel. Eve was tempted, and Adam chose to disobey by following her actions. Let us examine the nature of the temptation: the fruit was visually appealing (physical desire) and promised wisdom (possibly fueled by pride, covetousness, or emotional longing). Adam, on the other hand, received a direct command yet chose to rebel by doing the opposite. These details mirror many of our personal struggles, where unchecked desires often lead to poor choices. Take a moment to reflect on the past few years: your choices and the consequences that followed.

The reasons may vary, but self-awareness is the first step toward change. As the passage continues, we learn that their eyes were opened immediately after eating the fruit. For many of us, moments of realization do not happen instantly but they do come eventually.

You may recognize this pattern in your own life how you feel after repeatedly making the same choices. Even if only for a brief moment, most of us have felt the sting of regret or shame. It may happen after a relapse, speaking harshly to a loved one, or making a poor decision. Thankfully, God and often our loved ones can recognize when we have gone astray.

This is why God posed the question: "Where are you?" The purpose of this question was to lead them to self-awareness, accountability, and the recognition that they needed help. Are you always aware of where you stand emotionally, spiritually, mentally, and physically?

Often, the most honest answer is: "I do not know where I am, but I know I need help. I feel stuck." No matter what you are facing, bring it to God; He is patient, loving, compassionate, and truthful. When you surrender and acknowledge your current state, you allow yourself to be surrounded by people who can walk alongside you. The first step toward growth is honestly answering the question: Where are you?

ASK YOURSELF

* What was the true motivation behind my actions or decisions?

* Was it simply because it felt good in the moment?

* Did I believe it would improve something in me, make me feel accepted, or boost my confidence?

IT IS NOT JUST GOOD FOR YOU

GENESIS 17:19–21 *(NLT)*

*"But God replied, 'No—Sarah, your wife, will give birth to
a son for you. You will name him Isaac, and I will confirm
my covenant with him and his descendants as an everlasting
covenant. As for Ishmael, I will bless him also, just as you
have asked. I will make him extremely fruitful and multiply
his descendants. He will become the father of twelve princes,
and I will make him a great nation. But my covenant will
be confirmed with Isaac, who will be born to you and Sarah
about this time next year.'"*

Have you ever purchased a product with the same name as what
you wanted, only to discover that it was just one ingredient off?
The problem is that, even though it contains everything you need, that
single ingredient could be harmful to your health. Throughout life,
we will encounter people, opportunities, and choices that initially
seem like answered prayers but may ultimately lead us away from our
intended path.

This mirrors the story of Abraham and Sarah, the forebears of our faith. In Genesis 15:4, God promised Abraham a son through whom all the nations of the earth would be blessed. However, in a moment of frustration, Abraham succumbed to Sarah's suggestion to conceive a child with her maid, Hagar, leading to the birth of Ishmael. Given his old age, Abraham was content with Ishmael. Yet, God made it clear that Ishmael was not the promised covenant child. Even so, God still bestows blessings upon him. This illustrates that while Ishmael was still valued in God's eyes, he was not the one chosen to fulfill the divine promise. Ishmael was born out of human effort; appearing good on the surface, much like many choices we make in life. How often do we pause to seek God's guidance and discern whether something is truly His perfect will for us?

This applies to job offers, relationships, business ventures, school choices for our children, travel plans, and countless other decisions. Rather than relying on our own efforts to fulfill God's promises, why not embrace the wisdom of Romans 12:2? The Easy to Read Version states "don't change yourselves to be like the people of this world, but let God change you inside with a new way of thinking. Then you will be able to understand and accept what God wants for you. You will be able to know what is good and pleasing to him and what is perfect".

This transformation occurs through immersing ourselves in Scripture, which reveals how God sees, thinks, speaks, and acts. An imitation may appear genuine, but it is not the real thing. What seems good is not always what is best for you.

ASK YOURSELF

* Have I ever looked back and realized that something or someone, who once seemed good, was never truly meant for me?

If so, make it a habit to let God reshape your thinking and perspective—allowing you to make wiser, more fulfilling choices.

TRUSTING GOD

MATTHEW 6:27 *(ERV)*
"You cannot add any time to your life by worrying about it."

Life can easily overwhelm us as our minds become consumed with the cares of this world; what we will eat, wear, how our children are doing, who likes us, and countless other concerns. While these concerns are valid, the problem arises when they dominate our thoughts so completely that we become paralyzed, unable to move forward. For many, this mental overload has resulted in depression, anxiety, suicidal thoughts, and even physical health issues. That's why the theme scripture asks a powerful question: "Has worry added anything to your life?"

It's a question worth asking ourselves daily. This question serves as a grounding tool, helping us put our worries in perspective and manage their timing. Later in the passage, we are encouraged not to worry about tomorrow, but to face today's challenges one at a time because tomorrow will bring its own set of concerns. In essence, the verse teaches us to live in the present moment; practicing mindfulness.

The present is a gift; one we must unwrap and appreciate every single day. Verse 33 offers us a powerful formula to help reduce worry. If worry dominates your thoughts, it may be a sign that God is no longer at the forefront of your priorities. God can only guide us if we acknowledge Him and invite Him into our lives. Putting God first means filling our minds with His desires, His Word, His will, and His values; letting His character shape how we live. This is not a one-time act; it requires daily, intentional practice.

Life will inevitably bring storms; so what is your anchor in those moments? What Word are you using to fight back against the storm? What truth are you clinging to? What anchors your identity, even in the face of the lies your mind may speak?

In Deuteronomy 31:6 God instructed Joshua to be strong, courageous, and alert, unshaken by fear or intimidation, because He Himself was going before him. God promised that He would never fail nor forsake him. It may be difficult to believe this truth when you are in the midst of a storm. Therefore, I encourage you to consistently strengthen yourself with the scriptures shared in this entry as part of your daily routine. These verses will equip your mind to combat the negative thoughts and doubts that may arise.

ASK YOURSELF

* What other scriptures do I hold on to in times of challenge?

* Who can I turn to for spiritual support and encouragement?

Remember, "Give your entire attention to what God is doing right now, and don't get worked up about what may or may not happen tomorrow" Matt. 6:34 (MSG). Remember, one day at a time.

DANGERS OF SUCCESS AND FAILURE

PHILIPPIANS 3:12–13 *(NLT)*
*"I don't mean to say that I have already achieved these things
or that I have already reached perfection. But I press on to
possess that perfection for which Christ Jesus first possessed
me. No, dear brothers and sisters, I have not achieved it,but
I focus on this one thing: Forgetting the past and looking
forward to what lies ahead,"*

Life has no final arrival point; it is a continuous journey, not a fixed destination. Each of us is called to grow, develop, and stay focused on our divine purpose. As Benjamin Franklin put it "without growth, progress, such words as improvement, achievement, and success have no meaning."

Even when you discover your divine assignment, it is only a glimpse of the full purpose God has for your life. The next steps unfold as you continue walking in obedience along the journey. That is why the Apostle Paul reminds us in our theme scripture that despite his progress, he does not claim to have reached the finish line. Therefore, he urges us to let go of what's behind and press forward to what lies ahead.

Our main focus should be on what God has prepared for us and to keep striving toward it with purpose. But what does it really mean to forget what lies behind? It includes both our past victories and past struggles. Positive experiences may include achievements like staying clean for a stretch of time, saving money, improving a marriage, passing an exam, starting a business, or completing a major project. Negative experiences may involve regrets, failures, relapses, survivor's guilt, shame, repeated mistakes, or self-sabotage.

Dwelling too long on either the high or low points can paralyze our progress. This can lead to complacency or discouragement, both rooted in pride. That is why Paul encourages us to follow his example by releasing the past and pressing forward. This doesn't mean you ignore your past but you should not pitch a tent there or get stuck in it. Life's journey is long; so let us keep moving forward. Many people remain stuck at the place of their last major success or failure. Years later, they are still talking about the "last great thing" that happened.

Yesterday's testimony eventually loses its freshness; you cannot live off it forever. That could be why God did not allow the Israelites to store up manna in the wilderness. It was meant to be fresh daily. Others remain trapped in a moment of grief or past mistakes, unable to move forward. Without minimizing your experience, perhaps it is time to reframe how you view it so you can finally move forward.

How?

- Start with self-awareness; acknowledge where you may be stuck.
- Talk it through with a trusted person.
- Pray for guidance.
- Seek direction through God's Word, wise counsel, or even helpful books.
- Move forward with peace and clarity.

It may not be easy but with God's grace and the support of your community, you will get there.

One thing is certain: you must release the past.

ASK YOURSELF

- Am I ready?

WHAT IS THAT ANGER HIDING?

JONAH 4:4 *(NLT)*
"The Lord replied, 'Is it right for you to be angry about this?'"

Mark Twain once said, "Anger is an acid that can do more harm to the vessel in which it is stored than to anything on which it is poured." As many know, anger is often a secondary emotion; masking something deeper beneath the surface. Much like other habits, addiction, compulsive shopping, binge-watching, excessive social media, or self-sabotage, anger often serves as a shelter, hiding deeper issues like unforgiveness, pain, regret, or emotional wounds.

Surprisingly, many of these behaviors are actually subtle manifestations of unresolved anger in our lives. Anger can reveal itself in more than forty passive and aggressive forms; an eye-opening reality, is it not?

In this reflection, let us specifically focus on the link between anger and unforgiveness. Forgiveness, particularly self-forgiveness, has been a struggle for many of us at some point in our lives. If we are not careful, we can remain trapped in the toxic prison of unforgiveness: emotionally and spiritually. In our Scripture for today, Jonah would rather die than choose forgiveness. Have you ever found yourself in that place?

Unforgiveness can severely impact mental health and well-being; contributing to physical ailments, disturbed sleep, increased pain, fatigue, stress, and even heart issues. For the sake of your health: mind, body, and spirit; would it not make sense to begin letting go? God offers forgiveness the moment we repent and acknowledge our faults; sometimes even before we do. So why is it so hard to extend that same grace to ourselves?

Lewis B. Smedes once wrote, "To forgive is to set a prisoner free and discover that the prisoner was you." Forgiveness is not a one-time act; it's a journey, not a destination.

What to do:
1. Begin to unpack and process your emotions.

2. Make the decision to release them; it is, after all, a choice only you can make.

3. Then take the first step: journal, pray, seek therapy, or talk to someone you trust while showing yourself empathy and grace along the way.

ASK YOURSELF

(If you frequently struggle with anger)

* What might be hiding under the anger I feel?

* Could it be shielding unforgiveness, grief, fear, or emotional pain?

* Am I ready to explore the deeper issues that may have stunted my growth?

WHAT PART OF YOURSELF ARE YOU WILLING TO PART WITH?

MATTHEW 5:29–30 *(NLT)*

"So if your eye—even your good eye—causes you to lust, gouge it out and throw it away. It is better for you to lose one part of your body than for your whole body to be thrown into hell. And if your hand—even your stronger hand—causes you to sin, cut it off and throw it away. It is better for you to lose one part of your body than for your whole body to be thrown into hell."

Have you ever watched the movie *127 Hours?* If not, I highly recommend it. It powerfully illustrates the lengths a person will go to pursue what they desire and fulfill their life's purpose. The story follows a young man who embarks on a solo hiking trip without informing anyone of his whereabouts (his first mistake). During the journey, a boulder falls and traps his arm, leaving him immobilized. For five days, he remains trapped without food or water, forced to reflect deeply on his life while exploring potential ways to escape. Toward the end, he experiences a powerful vision of the life he could live, one worth fighting for. This vision fuels his decision to amputate his own arm in order to survive. That particular scene is difficult to watch, no matter how many times you have seen the film.

I often ask clients this thought-provoking question: "Do you think he knew from the beginning that amputation would be his only way out?" If you think about it, that boulder represents anything in our lives that keeps us stuck on the journey to our next; whether it is recovery, starting a business, working on your marriage, or something personal to you. So the question becomes: Why do we often wait so long to sever ties with the very thing we know is holding us back?

For some, that "boulder" may be negative thought patterns, fear, unforgiveness, grief, greed, attachment to the past, or prioritizing emotions over values. These things do not just block us from living a better life; they hinder us from walking in the divine purpose God originally designed for us. No matter how long you try to avoid it, there is ultimately only one way out: cutting off that harmful habit, mindset, or lifestyle that is keeping you bound.

Interestingly, our theme scripture, though primarily addressing adultery, parallels the climactic scene of this movie perfectly. If you think about it, clinging to a lifestyle outside of God's will is not so different from adultery; being unfaithful to the life He has called us to live.

That scripture urges us to cut off whatever part of our lives causes us to sin, reminding us it is better to lose a part than for our entire being to be thrown into destruction.

As you can see, the choice is yours. Remember, sin is anything that opposes what God has said and you do not have to die to experience hell; some people have been living in it for years. Hell can also be seen as a state of separation from God; a natural result of not following His direction for your life. However, separation from God does not mean He stops seeing you as His child. However, your emotions and choices may gradually lead you further from His presence, often without you realizing it.

ASK YOURSELF

* Where am I stuck?

* What needs to be cut off?

* What has been holding me back on my journey?

* What kind of help do I need and who can assist me?

If you are unsure, ask God to reveal it to you (Jer. 33:3).

INVENTORY/APPRAISAL

LUKE 14:28 *(NLT)*
"But don't begin until you count the cost. For who would begin construction of a building without first calculating the cost to see if there is enough money to finish it?"

Appraisal is the process of evaluating someone or something to determine its value, qualities, success, or needs (Dictionary.com, 2025). Self-appraisal is one of the most essential evaluations we can undertake. It allows you to assess how well you are doing, identify areas where you may be falling short, and determine what is needed for improvement.

Appraisal becomes especially crucial when you have a goal in mind; whether it is recovery, building a strong family, improving finances, growing a business, or passing an important exam. After all, how else can you know what is working and what is not?

It might help to view yourself as a business entity and ask:

- What is needed for this "business" to succeed?
- What will it cost me to make that happen?

In our theme scripture, Jesus outlines what is necessary before beginning any significant journey; whether becoming a disciple, a better parent, spouse, employee, friend, or pursuing sobriety. The core message is simple: "Do not start anything without first counting the cost."

Evidence that this advice is often ignored can be seen in the many "unfinished buildings" in our lives; goals started but never completed. Maybe you began your recovery journey, only to find that progress did not come as quickly as expected. Perhaps you have been working on yourself, yet your spouse has not acknowledged your efforts or made any noticeable changes. Maybe you have volunteered at work, but still have not received recognition or appreciation. You may be doing better as a parent, but it still feels like nothing is improving.

Each of these examples reflects a lack of preparation for the true cost of reaching your desired outcome.

- Do you have a habit of starting things, only to stop halfway because it became too difficult or progress seemed too slow?
- Did you truly evaluate everything needed for the journey?
- What did not work the last time?
- What might you do differently going forward?

From now on, for any project, especially your life, take the time to sit down and think things through carefully.

ASK YOURSELF

* Am I willing to see this through to the end, no matter what?

Also, ensure that whatever you pursue aligns with God's will for your life; otherwise, you may be creating unnecessary challenges for yourself. Another key part of self-appraisal is recognizing where we have fallen short and who we may have hurt along the way then repenting and seeking forgiveness wherever possible.

HONESTY

PROVERBS 11:6 *(CEV)*
"Honesty can keep you safe, but if you can't be trusted, you
trap yourself."

Honesty is a fundamental element of relationships and life overall. It goes beyond simply not lying; it involves speaking the truth, living the truth, and embracing the truth in all aspects (James E. Faust). Beyond attempting to deceive others, dishonesty reveals how disconnected you are from your own true self. When we fail to be honest, we often struggle to admit our mistakes, remain teachable, and stay open to correction and growth.

This, seemingly simple yet incredibly costly, habit has torn apart marriages, friendships, businesses, families, and more. Dishonesty makes it difficult for others to trust you, as they will constantly question what else you may be hiding. While trust is ultimately a choice others make, our honesty plays a significant role in their decision to take that chance on us. Where dishonesty exists, the person being dishonest will ultimately suffer the most over time. Dishonesty can result in isolation, as it becomes difficult for others to genuinely vouch for you.

Our theme verse reminds us that when we are untrustworthy, we trap ourselves. It is like unlocking a prison cell, only to lock yourself inside and expect others to release you. Your key to freedom lies in how honest you are with others. Be aware that when trust is broken due to dishonesty, it can take a long time, if ever, to rebuild. In essence, you will always have much to lose. Healing and recovery demand complete honesty with yourself, others, and God.

Paul urges us in Ephesians 4:17–25 to live as children of the light. If you identify with Christ and believe in God, you must understand that His Word is truth.

Jesus Himself is called the Truth and the Life. As you continue to abide in Him, and He in you (Jn. 15:5), you will discover more about what is true. You will learn to discard your old ways to embrace a better life by doing the following:

1. Allow the Holy Spirit to renew your thoughts and attitudes.

2. Surround yourself with honest individuals and remain open to being teachable.

3. Evaluate your life for areas of dishonesty, whether in your identity, behaviors, or other aspects.

4. Consider how much dishonesty has affected you in the long term.

*   Am I ready to change?

A helpful way to assess your honesty is to use Phillipians 4:8 (AMP) as a standard.

DO YOU LACK ANYTHING?

PSALM 23:1 *(AMPC)*
*"The Lord is my Shepherd [to feed, guide, and shield me], I
shall not lack."*

In today's world, one of the greatest fears many people face is the fear of lack, particularly the financial inability to provide for themselves. Among the many money mindsets out there, one common theme is rooted in the fear of lack, often stemming from past experiences of not having enough. This fear often shapes a particular lifestyle and approach to life. Truthfully, these lifestyles are not inherently wrong but when driven by fear, the motive can compromise the purity of the intention. It is not the desire for sufficiency that's the issue, but the fear fueling that desire.

Therefore, it is essential that we examine both our mindsets and our motives. In this reflection, let us also explore other overlooked aspects of lack. Though short, this verse is packed with meaning. I pray it brings revelation as you meditate on it. It begins by describing God as our Shepherd. A shepherd cares for, guides, shields, and protects always ensuring the safety and well-being of the flock. Simply put, a shepherd does not mismanage those entrusted to his care. Have you ever viewed God through this lens? When life gets hard, which lens do you tend to view Him through?

Here is a helpful check-in: ask yourself, Is God still God? Has He changed or been dethroned? If the answer is "no," then you can continue to trust Him at His word; He is still your Shepherd. Of course, this does not mean life will be without hardship.

Picture a shepherd in the field, and one of the sheep has wandered into a ditch as a heavy storm begins. The shepherd would most likely cover and protect that sheep, ensuring it does not drown in the storm. So when you find yourself in life's storms, picture your Shepherd, actively protecting and preserving you so you do not drown. 1 Corinthians 10:13 (TPT) reminds us that in life's trials, God filters their intensity, nature, and timing ensuring they're bearable. That is what a true Shepherd does and that is why Psalm 23:1 confidently declares, "I shall not lack." Lack here can apply to anything: finances, divine connections, favor, peace, health, joy, wisdom, strategies, or insight (feel free to add your own to the list).

More importantly, you will not lack His friendship, presence, love, counsel and even His rebuke, which is a sign of His love.

ASK YOURSELF

(So if I find myself lacking, I must ask:)

* Have I truly made God my Shepherd?

* What is my mindset?

* What are my motives?

* Where is my focus?

WHAT TYPE OF SOIL IS IT?

MATTHEW 13:3–8 *(NLT)*

"Listen! A farmer went out to plant some seeds. As he scattered them across his field, some seeds fell on a footpath, and the birds came and ate them. Other seeds fell on shallow soil with underlying rock. The seeds sprouted quickly because the soil was shallow. But the plants soon wilted under the hot sun, and since they didn't have deep roots, they died. Other seeds fell among thorns that grew up and choked out the tender plants. Still other seeds fell on fertile soil, and they produced a crop that was thirty, sixty, and even a hundred times as much as had been planted!"

According to the World Soil Information website, soil is the foundation of the ecosystem. It anchors, plants, roots and, stores the essential nutrients needed for growth (isric.org, 2025). I often compare humans to trees to illustrate this concept. In this analogy, the "soil" represents our hearts, which directly influence our growth or lack thereof.

In line with this idea, Jesus shared the parable known as *"The Parable of the Farmer Scattering Seed."* In the parable, a farmer scattered seeds across a field. Some landed on the path, some on shallow soil, others among thorns, and some on fertile ground. The outcome of each seed depended entirely on the type of soil it fell upon. The different types of soil in the parable symbolize the condition of our hearts when we receive information, counsel, correction, advice, and more. Before explaining the meaning behind each type of soil, Jesus revealed why He used parables: "They look, but they don't really see. They hear, but do not really listen or understand" (v.13).

Take a moment to reflect:
- Does this sound like me in certain areas of my life?
- Where do I look but fail to truly see?
- Could it be in complicated grief, anger, pride, or a toxic relationship?
- Where in my life have I heard, but not truly listened or understood?
- Could it be in my recovery journey, communication challenges, or relationships?

As we can see, the real issue is rarely the seed itself, but rather the soil on which it falls. Each soil represents a different kind of person. The wayside represents those who hear the message but fail to understand it. The rocky soil symbolizes those who receive the message with joy and excitement but lack deep roots and endurance to sustain growth. The thorny soil reflects those who hear the word but are quickly overwhelmed by the worries and distractions of life. The fertile soil stands for those who genuinely hear, understand, and patiently persevere until the message produces a fruitful harvest.

ASK YOURSELF

* Which type of soil best describes me and how has it affected my life overall?

* What kind of soil has received the seeds I have planted in others?

* How can I discern the condition of the hearts of those I interact with?

* Am I willing to pray that their hearts become fertile soil?

* Am I humble enough to cultivate and tend to the soil of my own heart?

Let Jesus walk with you through this journey. Surrender everything to Him especially if doing it your way has not worked so far.

YOU ARE THE LIGHT OF THE WORLD

MATTHEW 5:14–15 *(NLT)*
*"You are the light of the world—like a city on a hilltop that
cannot be hidden. No one lights a lamp and then puts it under
a basket. Instead, a lamp is placed on a stand, where it gives
light to everyone in the house.*

"There comes a time in the lives of those destined for greatness when we must stand before the mirror of meaning and ask 'why, having been endowed with the courageous heart of a lion, do we live as mice?'" (Brendon Burchard). Such a quote raises a few important questions:

- Are you truly destined for greatness?
- Do you recognize it?
- If yes, why are you living as a mouse?
- What does it mean to live as a mouse?

It means becoming comfortable with dysfunction and making excuses for toxicity in our lives. It is holding on to people, places, and things that no longer serve us, and resisting the call to grow simply because we have grown used to it (P. Debola Deji-Kurunmi).

I invite you to reflect:
- What areas of your life have you shrunk yourself?
- Where have you chosen to live small?

Our theme scripture reminds us that we are the light of the world; a light that cannot and should not be hidden. Just as a lamp is not lit to be placed under a basket, you are meant to shine where others can see and be impacted by it.

In this reflection, we will explore 'light' as both Jesus and as the unique gift God has deposited in you for your world. Once we have experienced Jesus; His salvation, peace, clarity, deliverance, and more, we are not meant to keep Him a secret. Make it a practice to share the good news you've received with others. You are, also, here to be a light; to reveal the vibrant colors of God within you to the world around you. You are a divine currency; uniquely valuable and deeply needed by many.

Now imagine how many more are waiting for you to shine at full brightness yet you keep dimming yourself to fit into every room you enter. I know life may have dealt you blows that made you feel like you have nothing to offer, like it is too late because of your past. I am here to remind you: You are the light of your world; wherever you are planted.

Give yourself permission to shine boldly every time the opportunity arises. Be the courageous lion you were made to be. Do not hide what God has placed inside you: your words, your counsel, the work of your hands. Be willing to release limiting mindsets, unhealthy places, toxic people, and dysfunctional patterns. Commit to the recovery and healing process even when it is hard.

ASK YOURSELF

* Am I aware of the light I carry? It might be joy, peace, fresh insight, wise counsel, strategy, comfort, or something more.

* Where have I dimmed my light over the years?

* Have others ever been amazed by something I said or did because of the depth of insight it carried?

THE NARROW GATE

MATTHEW 7:13–14 *(NLT)*
You can enter God's Kingdom only through the narrow gate.
The highway to hell is broad, and its gate is wide for the many
who choose that way. But the gateway to life is very narrow
and the road is difficult, and only a few ever find it.

The narrow gate echoes the road less traveled described by Robert Frost in his poem *"The Road Not Taken."* An anonymous quote reinforces this idea: "Those who take the road less traveled are the ones who discover the extraordinary." Choosing the road less traveled does not mean it is free of challenges, discomfort, or obstacles; yet, in spite of these, it leads to fulfillment, joy, and reward.

This idea is reflected in our theme scripture, which tells us that the gateway to life, God's Kingdom, is narrow, the road is difficult, and only a few ever find it. This means becoming a true follower: surrendering your ways and embracing His ways, acknowledging your trespasses, repenting, trusting Him, and cultivating a relationship with God;

otherwise, you risk missing the path entirely. In essence, what we seek is not handed to us; it must be pursued with intention and effort:

- How deeply do you desire it?
- Do you truly long to recover from addiction?
- Restore your marriage?
- Secure that job?
- Renew your body and mind?
- More importantly, how much do you desire to enter God's Kingdom?

The transformation you seek is reserved for those willing to go all in regardless of discomfort, setbacks, old habits, mocking voices, or opposition from others. If you want to experience something different, something extraordinary, you must commit to the work: surrender, recover, heal, and wholeheartedly embrace the new. A casual or lukewarm commitment will not suffice anymore. Do not miss your miracle and do not be late for your own life. Be humble enough to admit when you need help and ask for it.

In His mercy, God has given us the Holy Spirit to guide us through the journey. God, also, uses many different tools and people along the way if we are willing to let Him; it all begins with one step: surrendering and choosing to walk the road less traveled.

ASK YOURSELF

* Am I ready to make that decision today?

LUST

1 JOHN 2:16 *(MSG)*
*"Practically everything that goes on in the world—wanting
your own way, wanting everything for yourself, wanting to
appear important—has nothing to do with the Father. It just
isolates you from him."*

Matthew 6:22 tells us that our eyes are like lamps, lighting the way for our entire body. In other words, how we see the world shapes how we think, move, and behave. It is no surprise that lust is often called the 'sin of the eye,' in that what we fix our gaze on can trigger a powerful chain reaction in our thoughts and actions.

While commonly linked to sexual desire, lust can also refer to an intense craving for money, possessions, achievements, or even people. Lust objectifies; turning people, things, or ideas into tools for satisfying our personal cravings. What we often overlook is how lust impacts our brain chemistry, ultimately influencing our behaviors and decisions (Hanson, 2023).

Scripture highlights cravings like selfish ambition, materialism, and the desire for importance; each rooted in unchecked desire. These are all associated with this strong desire: lust. This can show up as impulsiveness, shortcuts to wealth, or a desire for results without the necessary effort. Ultimately, these cravings serve one purpose: to pull us further from God. At its core, lust stems from a lack of self-control and a self-centered mindset. True healing in this area is essential to deepen your relationship with God.

You cannot serve two masters; one will always be neglected. God will not compete for first place in your heart; you must willingly give Him that role. Have you genuinely surrendered your desires and cravings to God or are you still trying to 'help Him help you?' The truth is, without surrender, no one, not even your therapist, pastor, mentor, or God, can truly help you move forward. Once you surrender, the next step is learning to seek things for the right reasons or else you will keep ending up empty.

Surrounding yourself with accountability partners can greatly support you on this journey, but the most powerful tool for overcoming lust is shifting your focus. Romans 12:2 (MSG) urges us to fix our eyes on God; learn what He desires from us and respond quickly. We do this through consistent prayer, immersing ourselves in the Word, and serving others with love. Your future will be shaped by what fills your mind; its content and quality will either pull you closer to your purpose or further from it. Let us commit to reprogramming our minds by guarding what we see, hear, and allow into our spaces. You do have control over your mind, thoughts, emotions, and actions.

ASK YOURSELF

*   Will I take the reins or continue letting them steer my life?

77

VALUES

AMOS 3:3 *(NLT)*
"Can two people walk together without agreeing on the direction?"

Values serve as an internal compass, directing the course of our lives. They influence how we live; shaping our behavior, speech, thoughts, relationships, and even the situations we engage in. In essence, values are action-driven; what you value should be so clear in your life that others never have to question it. This means your values should guide your response to situations, not be dictated by them. Since we are relational beings, life inherently revolves around our connections with others. Therefore, value alignment becomes a critical component in our relationships.

When values are misaligned, it often leaves us with a sense that something is just not right. This is why the theme scripture asks, "Can two walk together unless they agree?" In other words, unless they are headed in the same direction.

If not, the journey may be rough. As you walk through recovery and healing, identifying your core values is essential. When followed with intention, your values will shape a daily action plan that reflects who you are and what you stand for. For example, someone who values family might make it a goal to be more present and engaged with loved ones. That may look like intentionally spending quality time with them or regularly checking in through phone calls.

They may also feel uneasy around people who disrespect or speak poorly about family. You can begin identifying your values by studying your own life; observing your habits and clarifying what truly matters to you. This process becomes clearer when guided by God's principles like Romans 12:2 (MSG), which encourages us to embrace God's will over cultural patterns. You can also discover your values by studying God's Word and praying for discernment about how His values align with your life.

All values have significance, but based on your unique divine design, certain values must take priority to help you walk your destined path. Reflect on your life; identify the values you have honored or ignored during pivotal moments.

ASK YOURSELF

* Do my values align with the people in my life?

* Am I heading the same way?

* Which values are essential for the life God has designed for me?

* Which values strengthen my relationship with God and those around me?

* What intentional steps can I begin to take to honor my values on a daily basis?

While values often fall into common themes, you should consistently evaluate them. If you are struggling to identify your values, a comprehensive list can be found by searching online for 'values list'.

BOUNDARIES

PROVERBS 4:23 *(TPT)*
"So above all, guard the affections of your heart, for they affect all that you are. Pay attention to the welfare of your innermost being, for from there flows the wellspring of life."

Boundaries can be a tricky topic, especially among believers; some argue they should not exist because of unconditional love, while others believe they are essential to prevent resentment and hurt from building in our hearts as we pursue unconditional love. Indeed, Scripture instructs us to love our neighbor as ourselves (Mk. 10:31).

However, to avoid harboring resentment or animosity, we must learn to guard the affections of our hearts, as they influence every aspect of who we are. We are urged to pay attention to the well-being of our innermost being, for from it flows the wellspring of life. According to the interlinear concordance, "to guard" means to watch over, preserve, and protect which is precisely what boundaries help us do.

As relational beings, we need community to thrive, which makes it crucial to learn how to navigate relationships in a healthy way. Although there are different types of boundaries, they all tend to impact the same area; our soul, including our emotions, mindsets, and imaginations. Deep soul wounds; such as trauma, being constantly relied upon, feeling isolated, or enduring dysfunction, often have lasting effects, even if we do not always recognize them. Have you experienced signs like unexpressed anger, walking on eggshells, venting to others, fatigue, poor sleep, irritability with loved ones, or wishing for change without taking action? (Bell, 2017). If yes, this highlights a lack of boundaries.

Boundaries help define what you are responsible for and what you are not (Gal. 6:2, 5). While we are encouraged to support one another, by listening, counseling, or simply being present, we are also called to take ownership of our own lives. In our efforts to be there for others, we sometimes unintentionally enable learned helplessness and truthfully, that is on us. I invite you to examine your relationships, even those closest to you.

We are commanded to love unconditionally, but that does not mean we must grant unconditional access to others. *"Granting unlimited access often leads to chaos and where chaos abounds, there is usually a lack of healthy boundaries"* (TerKeurst, 2022).

Let us look at two examples to help visualize this. In the first scenario, you lend money or pay bills for someone, but they repeatedly return because they are always in a financial bind. This may indicate that your financial boundaries need to be clarified.

Another example involves someone struggling with unresolved grief or emotional pain. Over time, they speak to you disrespectfully or act out, expecting you to rescue them. Though you are called to love, cultivating healthier relationships means addressing dysfunction in a way that honors God, yourself, and those around you. Sometimes, that means having difficult conversations but with love.

Remember: say what you mean, mean what you say but do not be mean. Love, also, involves helping others grow and mature even if they do not appreciate it at first, it will ultimately benefit them in the end.

ASK YOURSELF

* Have I noticed any dysfunction; perhaps the kind that would be obvious if I was watching it play out in a movie?

* Do some people seem to have full access to me: financially, emotionally, mentally, or physically, while showing little responsibility for that access?

* Has the behavior of those, around me, shown over time, that they are not able to handle the level of access I have given them?

SELF-LOVE

MARK 12:30–31 *(NLT)*

"And you must love the Lord your God with all your heart, all your soul, all your mind, and all your strength. The second is equally important: 'Love your neighbor as yourself.' No other commandment is greater than these."

Robin Sharma once said that true love for others can only come after mastering the art of self-love. So, what exactly is self-love especially considering that God commands us to practice it?

In our key scripture, Jesus highlights the two greatest commandments: to love God fully and to love others as we love ourselves. You may be tired of hearing, "You cannot truly love others until you know how to love yourself," but it remains a powerful truth. So, what makes loving ourselves so difficult at times?

In many ways, self-love is rooted in our identity: our self-concept. Over time, various experiences and influences have shaped our self-concept, which directly affects how we treat ourselves. We might constantly give to others; helping and being kind yet feel completely alone inside. This often stems from a lack of self-love, which is frequently tied to poor boundaries.

Self-love is the appreciation and care you extend to yourself through your actions, thoughts, and emotions. How we act, think, and feel should contribute to our growth; spiritually, emotionally, and physically. For many, the journey to self-love is a long and challenging one. For some, it begins with simply showing compassion toward themselves. It looks like asking ourselves, "What do I need right now?" and then acting on it.

Practice kindness toward yourself; treat your mistakes with grace, not punishment. Learn to walk away from dysfunction and set boundaries, so your love for others flows freely, not out of obligation. Additionally, becoming mindful of your thoughts and emotions; processing them without judgment and practicing positive self-talk, can greatly aid your journey.

Self-forgiveness is, also, key to self-love; it involves accepting where you are without shame or blame. Support is essential on the path to self-love. Who are the people in your life that can walk with you and help you heal in community? Self-esteem plays a vital role in self-love because it reflects how you see and value yourself.

Sadly, our self-perception is often distorted, largely because our perception of God is unclear. This takes us back to the first commandment: Love God with all your heart. It is difficult to love ourselves well if we don't understand who God is and how He sees us.

Above all, remember that God is love and everything else flows from that truth.

* Do I sometimes struggle to believe that God's love applies to me?

If so, you are not alone. But always remember, God is consistent and unchanging. He is good, He is able, He is willing to show up for you, and all that He does is perfect (Jas. 1:17–18). It may take time to fully embrace this truth, but extend compassion and grace to yourself along the way; that is the only true path to self-love.

JOY

GALATIANS 5:22 *(TPT)*
*"But the fruit produced by the Holy Spirit within you is divine
love in all its varied expressions: joy that overflows, peace that
subdues, patience that endures, kindness in action, a life full
of virtue, faith that prevails, gentleness of heart, and strength
of spirit."*

One of my favorite song lyrics is "The joy of the Lord is my strength." This powerful line is drawn from Nehemiah 8:10, where Nehemiah was encouraging his people. In this verse, Nehemiah urges us not to be discouraged or overwhelmed; no matter how bad things may seem because the joy of the Lord is our strength. That is right! It is not your own joy you must strive to find, but rather His joy that becomes your strength.

This divine joy can only be found in Him, as you choose to abide in His presence. This aligns with David's declaration: "In Your presence, there is fullness of joy" (Psa. 16:11). This tells us that God Himself is the source of joy because joy is what overflows in His presence. For a long time, there has been confusion between joy and happiness.

It is important to remember that happiness is often tied to current circumstances, making it conditional; whereas joy is a spirit. Joy is a fruit of the Spirit, which means it naturally flows from a life led by the Spirit of God. Our theme verse serves as a great indicator of how much we are allowing the Holy Spirit to lead our lives. Thankfully, this joy is not something we must strive to earn; it is birthed within us as we spend time with God.

So the question becomes: Are you spending enough time with God? Or are you too busy trying to manage everything on your own?

Joy reveals itself in your life even in the midst of difficult circumstances. When people spend time with you, can they sense that inner peace that radiates from joy, regardless of what you are facing? This fruit, joy, is essential in our healing and recovery journey because life won't always be smooth or easy.

ASK YOURSELF

* What do I do when life feels overwhelming?

* How do I tap into that joy?

First and foremost, surrender what is happening to God because it is beyond your control. Rely on Him. Spend time in His presence and within a community that reflects His love. Will it be quick and easy? Probably not. Rather, the key is to abide; staying with Him until you are filled with His joy.

HUMILITY

PHILIPPIANS 2:7–8 *(NLT)*
"Instead, he gave up his divine privileges; he took the humble position of a slave and was born as a human being. When he appeared in human form, he humbled himself in obedience to God and died a criminal's death on a cross."

Humility is a principle that often confuses many, as people struggle to find the right balance. Perhaps this confusion stems from viewing humility through the lens of society rather than its true source, God. True humility, as reflected in Philippians 2:7–8, is "knowing who you are, yet choosing to take a lower position out of obedience to God".

David Wilkerson stated that "a humble person is not one who thinks little of himself, hangs his head and says "I am nothing". Rather he is one who depends wholly on the Lord for everything, in every circumstance." Humility prompts the question: How am I expected to conduct myself in the context I'm currently in?

This mindset leads you to seek God's guidance in every area: how you dress, where to seek treatment, your choice of life partner, investments, friendships, sponsors, and more. Failing to rely on God in every area of your life is essentially pride. It is the "I got this" mentality.

C.S. Lewis said "the essential vice, the utmost evil is pride. Unchastity, anger, greed, drunkenness, and all that, are mere flea bites in comparison. It was through pride that the devil became the devil: pride leads to every other vice. It is the complete anti-God state of mind." This is the perfect opportunity to examine your life and identify any area where you have excluded God. Humility reflects character composure; it is what separates the mature from the immature.

A humble person remains a lifelong student, continually living out all seen in Proverbs 3:5–6. Several factors can hinder humility: greed, offense, isolation, people-pleasing, distorted identity, and lack of leadership composure (P. Debola Deji-Kurunmi). Humility is essential for where you are headed; it influences the transformation you desire in your family, marriage, recovery, emotional healing, and more.

Never forget: no matter what, you must remain obedient and actively engaged in what God is doing in your life. Be open to His help, guidance, and the people He has divinely placed in your life to walk alongside you. God has placed people in your path to help you, walk with you, and be a blessing. Humble yourself enough to receive them.

ASK YOURSELF

* Can I accept correction or rebuke and still recognize it as an
expression of love?

BUSYNESS OF LIFE

LUKE 5:16 *(NLT)*
"But Jesus often withdrew to the wilderness for prayer."

The way society is structured often makes it feel like there is never enough time to accomplish everything on our plates. Truthfully, you are not wrong; between work, school runs, visiting family, managing a business, personal projects, and pursuing your vision, life can feel overwhelming. It can seem impossible to get things done, especially if we consider slowing down as part of the process.

Here is the surprising truth: slowing down is actually the key to doing it all effectively. This is especially true when we slow down to spiritually refuel with and in God. Luke 5:16 reminds us that even Jesus withdrew regularly to pray and recharge after busy days of healing and teaching. Let us be honest, Jesus had a shorter timeline (just three years of ministry) and no modern transportation, yet He still prioritized rest. If we do not take intentional time to retreat, rest in the Lord, and care for our bodies, it is only a matter of time before we burn out or worse.

In His wisdom, God established a system of rest through the Sabbath commandment (Exod. 20:8–11). The Sabbath was designed as a sacred time for worship, rest, and connection with family. God's intention was not to burden us with another rule, but to instill the rhythm of rest and restoration in our lives. You might be trying to make up for lost years; whether due to addiction, unhealthy relationships, or constantly showing up for others while working on yourself. However, without a clear system of productivity, we will remain weary, resentful, and ultimately fall short of our intended goals. You simply cannot do and be everything all at once. Slowing down will look different for each person and each season. Still, it is essential to our overall well-being and quality of life.

So I invite you to take inventory of your life:

- Do I often feel aches, fatigue, or find myself falling sick more than usual?

- Am I constantly rushing from one thing to the next without any clear goals or schedule?

- Do I feel exhausted even after sleeping?

- Am I making frequent mistakes in different areas of my life?

If you answered yes to any of these, chances are you are running yourself into the ground.

ASK YOURSELF

* What needs to shift for my life to come into order?

* What does slowing down look like for me on a daily, weekly, monthly, or even yearly basis?

* What structure do I need to implement and who can help or hold me accountable?

Remember, your healing, recovery, transformation, and life outcomes are only as effective as the systems you build. So start building: wisely, prayerfully, and intentionally.

INTEGRITY (CHARACTER)

*"The integrity of the honest keeps them on track; the
deviousness of crooks brings them to ruin."*

Dwight D. Eisenhower stated "the supreme quality for leadership is unquestionable integrity. Without it no real success is possible, no matter whether it is on a section gang, football field, in an army, or in an office." Simply put, integrity is a powerful force. It is a vital character trait because it plays a crucial role in building strong relationships and fostering trust.

As social beings, this trait becomes even more essential for healthy and meaningful interactions. Our theme scripture reminds us that the integrity of the honest keeps them on the right path. It is good because your actions align with your words, and your outward behavior reflects your inner convictions.

A person of integrity adheres firmly to their core values, ensuring every aspect of their life aligns with those principles. You would not feel the need to change who you are depending on the environment or people around you.

That may be why David said in Psalm 101:6 (TPT) "my innermost circle will only be those I know are pure and godly. They will be the only ones I allow to minister to me." The ERV Version says "only those who can be trusted can live with me." The key word for me here is "innermost circle".

Truthfully, we all long for a steady, faithful, positive influence; someone who leads us closer to God and our divine purpose. But the question remains: Are we that person for others?

To live with integrity, you must live with the end in mind and that end should always reflect Christlike character. "Character development always involves a choice and temptation provides that opportunity" (Rick Warren). Emotions should not govern your choice but your values, anchored on the Word of God. Living with integrity demands a deep conviction about its importance in your journey of recovery, healing, and wholeness.

That is why integrity is also one of the core spiritual principles of Narcotics Anonymous (NA). Now, take time to assess your life: your choices, actions, words, and relationships and identify where integrity may have been lacking. Invite God into those areas; if He is not welcomed in them, you will continue to struggle to be used by Him and to walk in true success. This is the pruning process and it requires your full surrender. Will you embrace it?

ASK YOURSELF

* Have I genuinely upheld the principle of integrity in every area of my life?

* Have I engaged in relationships, whether business, friendship, or romantic, that compromised my internal values?

* How valuable have my words been in my life?

* When I say, "I have got you," or "I am always here for you," can people count on it, or was I simply saying what they wanted to hear?

Living with integrity ensures that you remain reliable and consistent, giving those around you no reason to question your actions.

SERVICE

ACTS 9:36 *(NLT)*
*There was a believer in Joppa named Tabitha (which in Greek
is Dorcas). She was always doing kind things for others and
helping the poor.*

Service is the intentional act of enhancing the quality of one's environment, often through giving back or paying it forward by helping others. Albert Einstein said "only a life lived for others is a life worthwhile." This perfectly described the life of Dorcas in our theme scripture.

Dorcas, a seamstress by profession, made a profound impact on her community through acts of kindness and service to the less privileged. She crafted clothes, coats, and other items for those in need. Dorcas exemplified the traits of a true servant: compassion, generosity, and selflessness.

While it is admirable to give others what you once received, it is even more powerful to go above and beyond in service to others. Maya

Angelou once said, "Among its benefits, giving liberates the soul of the giver." Service takes many forms depending on the context, whether it is toward family, friends, workplaces, neighborhoods, or broader communities. Dorcas's story illustrates how simply meeting a need can become a profound act of service. True service is about meeting a need with no expectation of personal gain. At home, service may look like doing chores but have you ever paused to ask your loved ones what they truly need from you?

Maybe what they need is a hug, respect, honest communication, forgiveness, or simply a heartfelt compliment. I hope this reflection stirs your heart and challenges you to grow in this area of your life. The key is intentionality. Colossians 3:23 states "whatever you do, work at it with all your heart as working for the Lord not for human masters." In doing so, you become God's hands extended to those around you. How often do others see the character of God reflected in you?

When you serve, the focus should shift from self to others. This outward focus can play a key role in your journey of healing, recovery, and restoration.

ASK YOURSELF

*   In this season, how can I serve?

FAITH

HEBREWS 11:1 *(AMPC)*
"Now faith is the assurance (the confirmation, the title deed) of the things [we] hope for, being the proof of things [we] do not see and the conviction of their reality [faith perceiving as real fact what is not revealed to the senses]."

Faith is deliberate confidence in the character of God whose ways you may not understand at the time (Oswald Chambers). This means your faith is rooted in what you believe about God's nature. If you believe God is trustworthy, unchanging, good, truthful, willing, and able; it becomes easier to stay grounded in faith. Believing in God's character is one thing, but faith also means trusting that His character is working in your favor.

Faith is a daily, intentional choice to trust God. Life's challenges often stir up doubt, fear, insecurity, and feelings of unworthiness. Faith is unnecessary for what you can already accomplish on your own. Faith declares: I will not attempt to control people or outcomes, but I trust that what I believe will come to pass, according to God's will.

What you believe must align with God's will and your divine purpose. This could involve your recovery, personal healing, restoration of family, or reconciliation in relationships. It may even be a God-inspired vision or project that feels far bigger than you. For me, one such leap of faith was writing this devotional which was never a plan. I wrestled with doubt, the imposter syndrome, and feelings of unworthiness, yet I clung to the unchanging truth of God's character. I stood firm on His Word, which assured me that He equips those He calls.

That is what it means to walk in faith: to obey, to trust, and to remain patient in the process, knowing that all things will work together for good. As our theme scripture reminds us, faith is the title deed, evidence of what we hope for and the assurance of what we do not yet see. Faith is spiritual perception; it transcends the physical senses and cannot be reasoned through logic alone. Are there areas in your life right now where you are actively standing in faith? Keep in mind that faith will be tested through trials, but those trials are meant to produce endurance and maturity (James 1:3-4).

Your perspective on trials and who you believe is behind them, will shape your faith and your capacity to receive (Jas 1:13).

A helpful tip: Never attribute your trials to God. Doing so can hinder your ability to receive from Him. Begin to thank God in advance for what you are believing for; regardless of what your current reality looks like. It will not always be easy, but you can rest in the promise that God will see you through. He has already made a way of escape available for you (1 Cor.10:13 TPT).

ASK YOURSELF

* What will my confession be months or years from now when my faith is tested?

* Will I complain, or will I boldly declare what I know to be true about God?

* Will I remind myself of the vision of recovery, healing, family unity and speak it aloud in faith?

TAKE OFF THE GRAVE CLOTHES

JOHN 11:44 *(NIV)*
*"The dead man came out, his hands and feet wrapped with
strips of linen, and a cloth around his face. Jesus said to them,
'Take off the grave clothes and let him go.'"*

As you come to the end of this devotional, my heartfelt prayer is that you will continue to welcome the guidance of God through the Holy Spirit as you walk through your healing, recovery, and restoration journey. This is truly a journey; one without a final destination.

Proverbs 4:18 reminds us that "the path of the just is like the shining sun, that shines ever brighter unto the perfect day." You have already received a measure of light, and as you continue walking with God, your light will shine even brighter; proportional to how much you rely on Him. This means that qualities such as understanding, peace of mind, trust, security, and purity will increase along the way.

Keep growing from faith to faith; it is a truly beautiful and transformative journey. After all, what could be better than having

God Himself as your guide? Do not be afraid; perfect love drives out fear (1 Jn. 4:18). Trusting in God's love will empower you to overcome fear, even in the face of challenges. Perhaps you are thinking, "I do not have that relationship with God yet," or "I'm not sure I belong to His family."

If so, I invite you to say the prayer at the end of this devotional. I also pray that you find a Bible-believing church that can walk alongside you on this journey.

Throughout this devotional, you have been called out of the spiritual graves you have been in; regardless of how long you were there.

Like Lazarus, I believe you have begun to wiggle your way into freedom. You might still be wrapped in some grave clothes but now is the time to begin shedding them. Picture it: a mummy still covered in wraps. It is hard, if not impossible, to remove those wrappings alone. That is why Jesus commanded the people in our theme Scripture to "take off his grave clothes and let him go."

Sometimes, we need others to help us remove the final remnants of what once held us down, even after Christ has already set us free.

We will need help loosening our mind (thoughts, beliefs), hands (productivity), and feet (direction) so we can begin to move freely.

ASK YOURSELF

* Do I have people around me who can help me remove the grave clothes now that I have been raised from spiritual powerlessness?

* Am I willing and ready to remove this final barrier standing between my new life and I?

I believe in you and more importantly, God believes in you and has your best interest at heart. Will you choose to believe in yourself and remain consistent on this journey?

Feel free to revisit any of the entries throughout your life; they are not meant to be read just once. The Holy Spirit may reveal something new you missed before, or offer fresh insight beyond what I shared.

Live a beautiful and blessed life, aligned with your original and divine design.

SALVATION PRAYER

If you have not given your heart and life to Christ, this is a good opportunity to do so. God reserves only good and perfect gifts for his children. Come into God's fold today; let Him help you on this journey to healing, recovery, and restoration so you can be the man or woman you should be. Let Him help you fulfill your destiny. If you are ready, just say this prayer aloud from your heart:

Lord Jesus, I come to you today, I acknowledge that I am a sinner in need of a savior. I believe that you came and died to save me. I open my heart to you and I confess with my mouth that you are my Lord and Savior from today onwards (Rom. 10:9-10).

Thank you, Lord, for saving me and transforming me; I am now born-again and I know my life will never be the same.

REFERENCES

American Psychiatric Association. (2013). *Diagnostic and statistical manual of mental disorders* (5th ed.). American Psychiatric Association.

Bell, C. (2017, September). Boundary starter kit.

Boland, M., & Hofstrand, D. (2021). *The role of the board of directors: Ag decision maker.* Iowa State University Extension and Outreach. https://www.extension.iastate.edu/agdm/wholefarm/html/c5-71.html

Cunnington, R. (2021, June 28). Neuroplasticity: How the brain changes with learning. *Science of Learning Portal.* https://solportal. ibe-unesco.org/articles/neuroplasticity-how-the-brain-changes-with-learning/

Derenzo, R. (2022, February 15). 7 habits of eagles leadership. *Dr. Derenzo's Blog.* https://cscslions.org/dr-derenzo-s-blog/7-habits-of-eagles-leadership-lesson

Hanson, R. (2023, June 7). The brain in lust and love. *Rick Hanson, PhD - Inner Strengths for Challenging Times.* https://rickhanson.com/brain-lust-love/

ISRIC - World Soil Information. (2025). Why are soils important? https://www.isric.org/discover/about-soils/why-are-soils-important

May, G. G. (1988). *Addiction & grace: Love and spirituality in the healing of addiction.* Harper San Francisco.

McCraty, R., & Childre, D. (2004). The grateful heart: The psychophysiology of appreciation. In R. A. Emmons & M. E. McCullough (Eds.), *The psychology of gratitude* (pp. 230–255). Oxford University Press.

National Council of Nonprofits. (2023). Board roles and responsibilities. https://www.councilofnonprofits.org/running-nonprofit/governance-leadership/board-roles-and-responsibilities

Narcotics Anonymous World Service Office. (1988). How it works. In *Narcotics Anonymous* (pp. 17–51). World Service Office, Inc.

TerKeurst, L. (2022). *Good boundaries and goodbyes*. Thomas Nelson.

INDEX

Old Testament (OT) Abbreviations

Traditional	Shorter	Full Name
Amos	Am	Amos
1 Chron.	1 Chr	1 Chronicles
2 Chron.	2 Chr	2 Chronicles
Dan.	Dn	Daniel
Deut.	Dt	Deuteronomy
Eccles.	Eccl	Ecclesiastes
Esther	Est	Esther
Exod.	Ex	Exodus
Ezek.	Ez	Ezekiel
Ezra	Ezr	Ezra
Gen.	Gn	Genesis
Hab.	Hb	Habakkuk
Hag.	Hg	Haggai
Hosea	Hos	Hosea
Isa.	Is	Isaiah
Jer.	Jer	Jeremiah
Job	Jb	Job
Joel	Jl	Joel
Jon.	Jon	Jonah
Josh.	Jo	Joshua
Judg.	Jgs	Judges
1 Kings	1 Kgs	1 Kings
2 Kings	2 Kgs	2 Kings
Lam.	Lam	Lamentations
Lev.	Lv	Leviticus

Mal.	Mal	Malachi
Mic.	Mi	Micah
Nah.	Na	Nahum
Neh.	Neh	Nehemiah
Num.	Nm	Numbers
Obad.	Ob	Obadiah
Prov.	Prv	Proverbs
Ps.	Ps	Psalms
Ruth	Ru	Ruth
1 Sam.	1 Sm	1 Samuel
2 Sam.	2 Sm	2 Samuel
Song of Sol.	Sg	Song of Solomon (Songs of Songs)
Zech.	Zec	Zechariah
Zeph.	Zep	Zephaniah

New Testament (NT) Abbreviations

Traditional	Shorter	Full Name
Acts	----	Acts of the Apostles
Apoc.	----	Apocalypse (Revelation)
Col.	Col	Colossians
1 Cor.	1 Cor	1 Corinthians
2 Cor.	2 Cor	2 Corinthians
Eph.	Eph	Ephesians
Gal.	Gal	Galatians
Heb.	Heb	Hebrews
James	Jas	James
John	Jn	John (Gospel)
1 John	1 Jn	1 John (Epistle)
2 John	2 Jn	2 John (Epistle)
3 John	3 Jn	3 John (Epistle)

Jude	----	Jude
Luke	Lk	Luke
Mark	Mk	Mark
Matt.	Mt	Matthew
1 Pet.	1 Pt	1 Peter
2 Pet.	2 Pt	2 Peter
Philem.	Phlm	Philemon
Phil.	Phil	Philippians
Rev.	Rv	Revelation (Apocalypse)
Rom.	Rom	Romans
1 Thess.	1 Thes	1 Thessalonians
2 Thess.	2 Thes	2 Thessalonians
1 Tim.	1 Tm	1 Timothy
2 Tim.	2 Tm	2 Timothy
Titus	Ti	Titus

About the Author

Josiane C. Somo walks in the intersection of healing and hope as both a licensed Mental Health Therapist and an Apostle called by divine purpose. While faith has been her foundation since childhood, it was in her darkest hour, contemplating suicide during her freshman year of college after losing her mother, that she encountered the transformative presence of Jesus Christ.

In that sacred moment, as despair threatened to consume her, Jesus took her hand with a promise that would forever change her life: "I will never let go." This divine encounter, which she would later discover echoed the very words of Scripture, ignited an intimate and intentional relationship with her Savior that continues to deepen today.

From that life-altering experience emerged her threefold calling: to reveal the boundless love of Jesus Christ, to guide others in discovering their true identity in Him, and to equip and mentor believers to step boldly into God's purpose for their lives.

This devotional represents her inaugural literary work, born from years of walking alongside others through their own seasons of brokenness and breakthrough. It is the first of many books to come, each one a testament to the God who holds our hands through every storm and never lets go.

Currently serving as a Mental Health Therapist, she continues to minister healing to hearts and minds while answering her apostolic call to advance the Kingdom of God through her writing, speaking, and mentoring ministry.